Four scary monsters
are going to the fair.

One scary monster
is flying in the air.

One scary monster
is going round and round.

One scary monster
is falling on the ground.

One scary monster
is scaring a big ghost.

Which scary monster
is being scared the most?

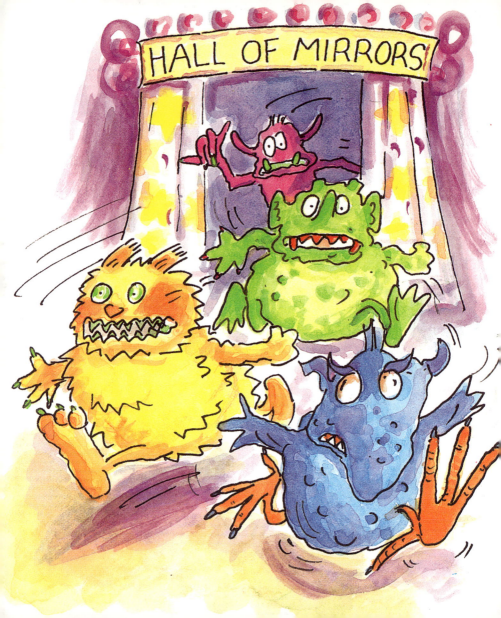